Alfred's

Music for Little Mozarts

Written Activities and Rhythm Patterns
to Reinforce Rhythm Reading

The *Rhythm Speller Book 4* reinforces rhythm skills based on the concepts introduced in the *Music Lesson Book 4*. The pages in the book correlate page by page with the materials in the *Music Lesson Book*. They should be assigned according to the instructions in the upper right corner of the pages in this book. They may also be assigned as review material at any time after the students have passed the designated *Music Lesson Book* page.

Each page of the *Rhythm Speller Book* has two activities—a **rhythm-writing** activity and a **rhythm-reading** activity. The written activities reinforce note values and counting through coloring, circling, drawing, or matching. The rhythm-reading activities help students practice:

• Clapping or tapping rhythm patterns while counting aloud.

• Playing rhythms on rhythm instruments or keys on the keyboard. (Other rhythm instruments can be substituted for those suggested throughout the book.)

• Chanting words based on rhythm patterns.

Alfred Music
P.O. Box 10003
Van Nuys, CA 91410-0003
alfred.com

ISBN-10: 1-4706-4053-8
ISBN-13: 978-1-4706-4053-8

Illustrations by Christine Finn

Christine H. Barden · Gayle Kowalchyk · E. L. Lancaster

Use with Alfred's Music for Little Mozarts,
Lesson Book 4, page 5.

Rhythm Writing

Circle each rhythm pattern in ¾ time.

Draw a line through each rhythm pattern in 4/4 time.

Rhythm Reading

1 Clap and tap the rhythm pattern. Tap notes with a down stem (♩) on your lap.

Clap notes with an up stem (♩). Count aloud.

Count: 1   1   1   1   1   1   1 - 2   1   1   1   1   1   1   1 - 2

2 Play the above rhythm pattern with a tambourine.

Rhythm Writing

1 Circle the notes that get 1 count with a **red** crayon.

2 Circle the notes that get 2 counts with a **blue** crayon.

3 Draw an **X** through the notes that get 3 counts.

Rhythm Reading

1 Clap and count the rhythm pattern.

Count: 1   1   1   1   1   1   1 - 2 - 3   1 - 2 - 3

2 Using finger 3 of the RH, play the above rhythm pattern on
Then, play again with RH finger 2.

Rhythm Writing

Use with page 8.

1 Circle the rhythm pattern ♩♩♩♩ | ♩♩ 𝅗𝅥 ‖ with a **blue** crayon.

2 Circle the rhythm pattern ♩♩𝅗𝅥 | 𝅝 ‖ with an **orange** crayon.

3 Circle the rhythm pattern 𝅗𝅥 𝅗𝅥 | ♩♩♩ 𝄾 ‖ with a **gray** crayon.

Rhythm Reading

1 Clap and count the rhythm pattern.

Count: 1   1   1   1   1   1   1 - 2   1   1   1 - 2   1 - 2 - 3 - 4

2 Using finger 2 of the RH, play the above rhythm pattern on
Then, play again with RH finger 3.

Rhythm Writing

Draw a line connecting the dots to match the rhythm patterns to their counts.

$\frac{3}{4}$ ♩ ♩ | ♩. ‖ •   • 1 - 2 - 3 | 1 - 2 - 3

$\frac{3}{4}$ ♩. | ♩. ‖ •   • 1 1 1 1 | 1 1 1 - 2

$\frac{4}{4}$ ♩ ♩ ♩ ♩ | ♩ ♩ ♩ ‖ •   • 1 - 2 1 | 1 - 2 - 3

Rhythm Reading

Clap and count the rhythm patterns.

❶

$\frac{3}{4}$ ♩ ♩ ♩ | ♩. | ♩ ♩ ♩ | ♩. ‖

Count: 1   1   1   1 - 2 - 3   1   1   1   1 - 2 - 3

❷

$\frac{4}{4}$ ♩ ♩ ♩ ♩ | ♩ ♩ ♩ | ♩ ♩ ♩ | 𝅝 ‖

Count: 1 1 1 1   1   1   1 - 2   1   1   1 - 2   1 - 2 - 3 - 4

❸ Play each rhythm pattern (1–2) with a hand drum.

Use with page 11.

Rhythm Writing

Draw a **dotted half note** in each box.

Then, clap and count the rhythm pattern.

Example:

Rhythm Reading

Tap the rhythm pattern on your lap. Tap notes with a down stem (♩) with your LH.

Tap notes with an up stem (♩) with your RH. Count aloud.

1
RH

LH
Count: 1 - 2   1   1 - 2 - 3   1   1   1   1 - 2 - 3

2
RH

LH
Count: 1   1   1   1 - 2 - 3   1 - 2   1   1 - 2 - 3

Rhythm Writing

Draw a line connecting the dots to match each rhythm pattern to its correct time signature.

Rhythm Reading

Clap the *Puccini Pooch* rhythm pattern and chant the words.

Chant: Puc - ci - ni   Pooch

Use with page 15.

Rhythm Writing

Draw a line connecting the dots to match the rhythm patterns to their counts.

Rhythm Reading

1 Using finger 3 of the RH, play the rhythm pattern on and count aloud.

Count: 1 - 2   1 - 2   1   1   1   rest   1   1   1   1   1   1   1   rest

2 Using finger 3 of the LH, play the rhythm pattern on and count aloud.

Count: 1 - 2   1   1   1   1   1 - 2   1   1 - 2 - 3

Rhythm Writing

Draw a line connecting the dots to match each rhythm pattern to its correct time signature.

Rhythm Reading

Clap and count the rhythm patterns.

1

Count: 1   rest   1   rest   1   1   1   rest   1   1   1   1   1   1   1   rest

2

Count: 1   1   1   1 - 2 - 3   1 - 2   1   1 - 2 - 3

Use with page 19.

Rhythm Writing

1 Circle the rests that get 1 count with a **red** crayon.

2 Circle the rests that get 2 counts with a **blue** crayon.

3 Circle the rests that get 4 counts with a **green** crayon.

Rhythm Reading

1 Tap the rhythm pattern on your lap. Count aloud.

Count: 1   1   1   **rest**   1   1   1   **rest**   1   **rest**   1   **rest**   1 - 2 - 3 - 4

2 Using finger 3 of the LH, play the above rhythm pattern on
Then, play again with LH finger 2.

Rhythm Writing

Draw a line connecting the dots to match the rhythm patterns to their counts.

Rhythm Reading

Clap and count the rhythm patterns.

1

Count: 1   rest   1   rest   1   1   1   rest   1   1   1   1   1   1   1   rest

2

Count: 1   1   1   1   1 - 2   1 - 2   1   1   1   1   1   1   1 - 2

3 Play each rhythm pattern (1–2) with bells.

Use with page 23.

Rhythm Writing

Draw a line connecting the dots to match each rhythm pattern to its correct time signature.

Rhythm Reading

Tap the rhythm pattern on your lap. Tap notes with an up stem (♩) with your RH.

Tap notes with a down stem (♩) with your LH. Count aloud.

Count: 1   1   1   1   1 - 2   1 - 2   1 - 2   1 - 2   1 - 2   1 - 2

Rhythm Writing

Draw a line connecting the dots to match the rhythm patterns to their counts.

Rhythm Reading

1 Using finger 2 of the RH, play the rhythm pattern on Count aloud.

Count: 1   1   1   1   1 - 2   1 - 2   1   1   1   1   1 - 2 - 3 - 4

2 Using finger 3 of the LH, play the rhythm pattern on Count aloud.

Count: 1   1   1   1 - 2 - 3   1 - 2   1   1 - 2 - 3

Use with page 27.

Rhythm Writing

Circle each rhythm pattern in $\frac{3}{4}$ time.

Draw a line through each rhythm pattern in $\frac{4}{4}$ time.

Rhythm Reading

Tap the rhythm pattern on your lap. Tap notes with an up stem (♩) with your RH.

Tap notes with a down stem (♩) with your LH. Count aloud.

Count: 1   1   1   1 - 2 - 3   1   1   1   1 - 2 - 3

Rhythm Writing

Clap the rhythm patterns. Then, draw a line to match each rhythm pattern to the music friend whose name matches the rhythm.

Nan-ne-rl Mouse

Pach-el-bel Pen-guin

J. S. Bun-ny

Rhythm Reading

❶ Clap and count the rhythm pattern. Count aloud.

Count: 1   1   1   1   1   1   1 - 2   1 - 2 1 - 2   1 - 2 - 3 - 4

❷ Using finger 1 of the LH, play the above rhythm pattern on
   Then, play again with LH finger 2.

Rhythm Writing

Use with page 31.

1 Circle the rhythm pattern $\frac{3}{4}$ 𝅗𝅥 ♩ | 𝅗𝅥. ‖ with a **blue** crayon.

2 Circle the rhythm pattern $\frac{4}{4}$ ♩ ♩ ♩ ♩ | 𝅗𝅥 𝅗𝅥 ‖ with an **orange** crayon.

3 Circle the rhythm pattern $\frac{4}{4}$ ♩ ♩ ♩ ♩ | 𝅝 ‖ with a **purple** crayon.

Rhythm Reading

1 Clap and tap the rhythm pattern. Clap notes with an up stem (𝅗𝅥.).
Tap notes with a down stem (♩) on your lap. Count aloud.

Clap   *Tap on lap*

$\frac{3}{4}$ 𝅗𝅥. | 𝅗𝅥. | ♩ ♩ | ♩. ‖

Count: 1 - 2 - 3   1 - 2 - 3   1 - 2   1   1 - 2 - 3

2 Using finger 2 of the RH, play the above rhythm pattern on
Then, play again with RH finger 3.

Rhythm Writing

Clap the rhythm patterns. Then, draw a line to match each rhythm pattern to the music friend whose name matches the rhythm.

Moz-art Mouse

El-gar E. El-e-phant

Puc-ci-ni Pooch

Rhythm Reading

1 Clap and tap the rhythm pattern. Tap notes with a down stem ( ) on your lap.

Clap notes with an up stem ( ). Count aloud.

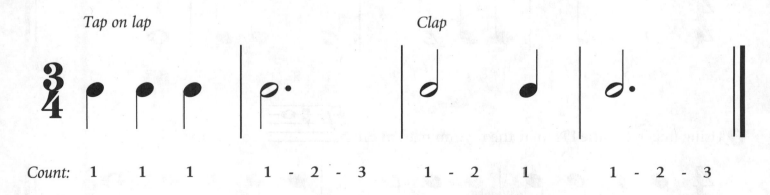

Tap on lap   *Clap*

Count: 1   1   1   1 - 2 - 3   1 - 2   1   1 - 2 - 3

2 Using finger 2 of the LH, play the above rhythm pattern on 𝄢 Then, play again with LH finger 3.

Use with page 35.

Rhythm Writing

Draw a line connecting the dots to match the rhythm patterns to their counts.

Rhythm Reading

1 Using finger 2 of the RH, play the rhythm pattern on Count aloud.

Count: 1 - 2   1 - 2   1   1   1 - 2   1 - 2   1   1   1 - 2 - 3 - 4

2 Using finger 2 of the LH, play the rhythm pattern on Count aloud.

Count: 1   1   1   1   1   1   1 - 2   1   1   1   1   1 - 2 - 3 - 4

Rhythm Writing

Draw a line connecting the dots to match each rhythm pattern to its correct time signature.

Rhythm Reading

Tap the rhythm pattern on your lap. Tap notes with an up stem (♩.) with your RH.

Tap notes with a down stem (♩) with your LH. Count aloud.

Count: 1 - 2 - 3   1 - 2 - 3   1 - 2   1   1 - 2 - 3

Use with page 39.

Rhythm Writing

1 Change each **whole note** to a **quarter note** by coloring it **black** and drawing a stem on the right.

2 Change each **half note** to a **dotted half note** by adding a dot on the right.

3 Then, clap and count the rhythm.

Rhythm Reading

Clap and count the rhythm patterns.

1

Count: 1   1   1   1   1 - 2   1 - 2

2

1 - 2   1 - 2   1 - 2 - 3 - 4

3

1 - 2   1 - 2   1   1   1 - 2

4

1   1   1   1   1   1   1 - 2

5 Play each rhythm pattern (1–4) with bells.

Rhythm Writing

Draw a line connecting the dots to match the rhythm patterns to their counts.

Rhythm Reading

Tap the rhythm pattern on your lap. Tap notes with a down stem (♩) with your LH.

Tap notes with an up stem (♩) with your RH. Count aloud.

Count: 1 - 2   1 - 2   1   1   1 - 2   1   1   1   1   1   1   1 - 2

Use with page 43.

Rhythm Writing

Draw a line connecting the dots to match each rhythm pattern to its correct time signature.

Rhythm Reading

Clap and count the rhythm patterns.

1

Count: 1   1   1   1   1 - 2   1 - 2   1   1   1   1   1 - 2 - 3 - 4

2

Count: 1   1   1   1 - 2 - 3   1 - 2   1   1 - 2 - 3

Rhythm Writing

Draw a line connecting the dots to match the rhythm patterns to their counts.

Rhythm Reading

Play each rhythm pattern with rhythm sticks. Count aloud.

1

Count: 1   1   1   1   1 - 2   1 - 2   1   1   1   1   1   1   1 - 2

2

Count: 1 - 2 - 3   1 - 2 - 3   1 - 2   1   1 - 2 - 3

3 Play each rhythm pattern (1–2) on a wood block.

Rhythm Writing

Use with page 47.

Clap the rhythm patterns. Then, draw a line to match each rhythm pattern to the music friend whose name matches the rhythm.

Pro-fes-sor Hay-dn Hip-po

ni-na Bal-le-ri-na

Bee-tho-ven Bear

Cla-ra Schu-mann-Cat

Rhythm Reading

1 Using finger 2 of the RH, play the rhythm pattern on Count aloud.

Count: 1 - 2 - 3   1   1 - 2 - 3   1   1   1   1   1   1 - 2 - 3 - 4

2 Using finger 3 of the LH, play the rhythm pattern on Count aloud.

Count: 1 - 2   1   1   1   1   1   1 - 2   1   1 - 2 - 3